SYSTEMIZE, AUTOMATE, DELEGATE

Systemize, Automate, Delegate

How to Grow a Business
While Traveling, on Vacation,
and Taking Time Off

Tom Corson-Knowles

Copyright © 2013, 2014 by Tom Corson-Knowles

All rights reserved.

No part of this publication may be reproduced, distributed, or transmitted in any form or by any means, including photocopying, recording, or other electronic or mechanical methods, or by any information storage and retrieval system without the prior written permission of the publisher, except in the case of very brief quotations embodied in critical reviews and certain other noncommercial uses permitted by copyright law.

Published by TCK Publishing.

www.TCKPublishing.com

Arial & Cambria fonts used with permission from Microsoft.

Get the free newsletter for more marketing tips at:

www.BlogBusinessSchool.com

Earnings Disclaimer

When addressing financial matters in any of our books, sites, videos, newsletters or other content, we've taken every effort to ensure we accurately represent our products and services and their ability to improve your life or grow your business. However, there is no guarantee that you will get any results or earn any money using any of our ideas, tools, strategies or recommendations, and we do not purport any "get rich schemes" in any of our content. Nothing in this book is a promise or guarantee of earnings. Your level of success in attaining similar results is dependent upon a number of factors including your skill, knowledge, ability, dedication, business savvy, network, and financial situation, to name a few. Because these factors differ according to individuals, we cannot and do not guarantee your success, income level, or ability to earn revenue. You alone are responsible for your actions and results in life and business. Any forward-looking statements outlined in this book or on our Sites are simply our opinion and thus are not guarantees or promises for actual performance. It should be clear to you that by law we make no guarantees that you will achieve any results from our ideas or models presented in this book or on our Sites, and we offer no professional legal, medical, psychological or financial advice.

Some of the URLs (excluding any and all URLs to Amazon sites) in this book may be affiliate links. This means if you go to the URL and purchase the item, I may receive an affiliate commission. Please understand I only recommend products or services I use personally and believe will add tremendous value to my readers. I am disclosing this in accordance with the Federal Trade Commission's 16 CFR, Part 255: 'Guides Concerning the Use of Endorsements and Testimonials.'

Contents

Why I Wrote This Book ix

Chapter 1 The System 1

Chapter 2 Systemize 9

Chapter 3 Automate 29

Chapter 4 Delegate 35

    Systemization Phase 1 Research 45

    Systemization Phase 2 Plan 51

    Systemization Phase 3 Implement 57

    Systemization Phase 4 Review 59

    Systemization Phase 5 Repeat 61

Chapter 5 Solving The Big Problems After Systemization 63

Chapter 6 Ninja Business Tools and Tricks 67

Bonus! Free Video Course for Growing Your Business 83

Connect With The Author 85

About The Author 87

Other Books By Tom Corson-Knowles 89

Index 91

WHY I WROTE THIS BOOK

About 3 months after moving in with my fiancé, I realized I would have to start paying all the bills for her—rent, food, gas, shopping (a lot of shopping), travel, and numerous new household goods I never knew I needed, like a massage chair (which is now my favorite chair, despite my earlier objections).

I always lived well below my means as I grew my first lifestyle business in college and it was a shock to me to find out someone could spend so much money so fast on clothing and "totally unnecessary items," as I kept reminding her. The universe works in mysterious ways, and I happened to fall in love with a woman who knows how to spend a lot of money, and does a very good job at it. At first, I thought that even if I earned more money, she would just spend it all with her insatiable appetite for more luxuries!

Well, I can honestly say that it was the best thing that ever happened to me financially. She forced me to stretch myself. I had gotten comfortable living a modest lifestyle on my own and my business stopped growing as fast as it had before because I got complacent (*read: lazy*).

I stopped doing the things in business that had made me so successful in the first place, a devastating mistake business owners often make. Luckily, she snapped me out of my complacency when I saw the massive credit card bills each month. I started a new business, refocused my efforts, and my income grew faster than I ever thought possible. Everything seemed to be going perfectly!

A few weeks later, my fiancé told me that she had two cousins getting married about two months apart—one in the Philippines and one in South Africa—and that we had to go to both weddings! Not only that, but since we had to travel all around the world to go to the weddings, we might as well travel around Asia and Africa and have some fun while we were there for 90 days or so.

"*Really?*" I said incredulously when she gave me the news.

Just when I thought I had my business and financial life back on the fast track to financial freedom, I found out I would have to spend a fortune on plane tickets, hotels and other travel costs, and I would be away from my business for 3 months! I felt like every time I moved a step ahead, life was pushing me back down. Have you ever felt like that?

Again, it took me a while but I eventually realized that this, too, was a blessing in disguise. Remember that old saying, "This too shall pass"... I had to change it to, "This too is a blessing." And so it is.

When I first went into business several years ago, here was my major financial goal, to:

> *Earn $10,000 a month in residual income from my businesses and be able to do whatever I want, whenever I want, wherever I want with whomever I want.*

I realized that I had achieved the first part of the goal—earning more than $10,000 a month from my businesses, but I was falling far short on the whole doing whatever I want thing. I felt stuck in my business. I worked EVERY day. And I mean EVERY day. Even if we went on a 12 mile hike and had to get up at 5am to leave and didn't get home until midnight, I'd get up even earlier or stay up late and work.

I'll be the first to admit that my good work ethic and work habits are what helped me grow my business so fast. I remember when I used to be lazy and work less than 10 hours a week because I was already earning enough money to get by and save a few thousand dollars a month. I had to change those old work habits to grow my income a lot faster. But now my work habits had become the problem—I was addicted to work and couldn't let go of it.

Sometimes in life, you must realize it's time to evolve and change once again. It's time to grow to a new place, a whole new level of success, whatever success means to you.

As Aristotle said, "We are what we repeatedly do. Excellence, then, is not an act, but a habit." I had the habit of being an excellent worker, and it earned me a great income in business. But now I had to learn how to build an excellent business and get me out of the day-to-day management of my business so that it could grow without me and I could live the lifestyle of my dreams on a 90-day trip around the world with the love of my life.

In this book, I'm going to share with you how I did it. You will learn:

- ☑ *How I changed my old work habits and took 3 months off work without major withdrawals, stress or losing my income*
- ☑ *How I set my business up for success on my trip so that it would grow without me while I enjoyed my travels*
- ☑ *How I grew my business by over 37% in 3 months on my trip*
- ☑ *How I made sure my customers were happier than ever before*

And, even more importantly, I'm going to share with you WHY you must systemize your business so that you can grow your business even faster, help more people, and have more free time to do what you love in life.

Ready to get started? Let's go!

Chapter 1

The System

First of all, you have to realize that a business is nothing more than a series of processes—four essential processes to be exact. And each of these business processes have key tasks that must be completed in a certain way to keep the business running well.

For example, if you own a restaurant, here is the simplified breakdown of crucial business processes in a typical restaurant business:

Marketing

Marketing is how you attract new and repeat customers. For a restaurant, this might mean having a website, being listed in Yelp and Google Maps, having an ad in the local newspaper or TV station, social media marketing, search engine optimization, creating branded apparel, gifts, gift cards and other marketing strategies.

The goal of marketing is to get new customers to buy from you and old customers to keep buying from you. The end goal of marketing is NOT to get more traffic to a website or more people window-shopping. You want new buyers and repeat buyers!

Customer Service

Customer service is about how you take care of your customers needs and help them solve their problems.

Let's be honest; most customer service SUCKS these days! That's why even just tiny improvements in your company's customer service could dramatically improve your customer loyalty and profitability. Because even doing something simple like returning a phone call the same day can set you apart from the big businesses that are completely bureaucratic and care about their customers enough to leave them waiting on hold for hours with poorly trained customer service people.

For a restaurant, customer service includes tasks such as seating customers, taking orders and how you deliver the food.

Financial Management

Financial management is how the company manages its money. Financial management is first and foremost about managing cash. Some companies look "profitable" on their income statement but they have horrible cash flow—that's a good way to go bankrupt.

For a restaurant, financial tasks would include collecting money from your customers, paying bills, paying taxes, managing cash flow, and investing in new materials, inventory and products.

Operations

Operations is how you create and deliver your product to your customer. Operations is all about execution. It's getting done the work that you planned to do ahead of time.

For a restaurant, this includes preparing the food for your customers and delivering it to them in a timely manner.

* * *

These are the only four essential processes or components in a business. You might think of some other pieces to the business pie, but none of them are crucial. These are the elements that must be present for any business to function and grow.

Here are some other business processes that you might think are crucial but really aren't:

RESEARCH AND DEVELOPMENT (R&D)

Although R&D is a very important part of business, it's not crucial in the short term for most businesses. You can easily have a business run and be profitable without any R&D. Forever? Of course not. But any good business will run for a few months just fine without any R&D while you travel the world on vacation.

In the long term, R&D is one of the key parts of your business that will either separate you from the competition or not. And failure to separate yourself from the competition means your product offering becomes a commodity and your margins and sales diminish. Investing in R&D is a long-term business strategy so it is very important for long-term success.

The only constant in business is change, and every business must innovate to stay add value to its customers. The end goal of this innovation is to create new products and services and better strategies. Systemizing, automating and delegating your business will give you much more free time to focus on innovation and reap the long term rewards of having more free time and more money.

Managing Employees

My business doesn't even have any employees, and I'm going on a 90-day vacation so that just proves that you don't need to manage employees to have a profitable business.

You will have to manage a team, however, and that is similar but different.

Sales

To me, sales is simply a sub-category of marketing. But if you want to call it the 5th essential business process, I'd let it slide.

Systemize, Automate, Delegate

Now that you understand the four essential business processes, it's time to understand how to systemize, automate and delegate these processes so that your business works without you.

Organization Is Key

The biggest reason most entrepreneurs fail isn't because of a lack of capital. It's because of a lack of organization! The better you organize your money, the more money will flow to you. Businesses that are highly organized and efficient in their management of money tend to grow. Businesses that fail to organize their money will go bankrupt sooner or later, or, at the very least, suffer major financial losses.

That's why serious investors always want to see a business plan before they invest in a business. It's not because they think that your financial forecasts are perfect. It's because they know that if you don't have a clear plan for how you're going to use their money, there will be far safer and more profitable places to put their money to work. Organization reduces risk. And lower risk means more predictable business earnings. And more predictability is very valuable to investors, business owners and customers.

This entire book is really a book on organization for business owners. You will be learning how to organize every single aspect of your business from your marketing to operations to finances and everything in between. Some of the exercises in this book may seem tedious and boring. That's because you're used to doing all the work yourself and have no real system for your business!

Trust me, it's a lot more fun to spend a week systemizing your entire business and then have other people run it for you and grow it to be an international powerhouse than it is to run the business by yourself with no system or organization and struggle financially for the rest of your life.

Well, the choice is yours; would you rather have an organized, profitable, growing business or a disorganized business that keeps you trapped financially, working frantically for the rest of your life?

Systemization isn't just some buzzword or academic theory of business management. Systemization works. It's what every successful business does and what most unsuccessful businesses fail to do well.

And you don't need an MBA or Harvard degree to understand it. Systemization can be as simple as creating a checklist for your employees to use when completing certain tasks. But these systems save time and money and increase quality. For example, pilots use checklists every time before taking off. Imagine if they didn't. What if they forgot step 7 on the checklist and took off and the plane crashed? That would be completely unacceptable! And that's why checklists are mandatory in aviation.

But every single day across the world businesses crash because the entrepreneurs in the pilot seat failed to create checklists and systems to keep the business running safely and smoothly. Let's be honest: starting, owning and running a business is inherently risky. Creating the right systems is what helps you manage the risk. And risk management is incredibly important. I'd rather invest in someone who understands risk management than someone who only knows how to take risks and get lucky because in the long run the risk manager will be wealthy while the lucky risk-taker will be broke.

Another huge benefit of systemizing is that when business tasks and processes such as customer service are systemized, *any competent person can then do those tasks*. When you haphazardly run your business without any system, no one knows what's going on! That means it's difficult, if not impossible, for other people to help manage business processes and tasks and help you grow your business.

The #1 most important thing you can do to grow your business is to organize it and systemize it. It's more efficient, meaning it will save you time and money, and it will get a better, more consistent result, meaning you can charge higher prices to customers because you'll be delivering higher value. So systems increase your revenue and reduce your costs—what more could you possibly want for your company?

In business school management classes, I remember my professors telling me that employees are the greatest asset of a business. But that's not true! You could hire the best employees in the world, but if there's no organization or system for them to work with, they won't be very productive. The same holds true for contractors. This is why many entrepreneurs can't "afford" to hire high quality contractors. They have no system for the business so the results they get from paying $500 or $5,000 for a contractor are poor at best. On the other hand, entrepreneurs with highly organized and systemized businesses can afford to hire the best contractors at a higher but fair price and profit handsomely from that exchange. The difference isn't the contractor or employee—the difference is the level of organization and systemization of the business itself. And it's the entrepreneur's job to organize and systemize in order to make a profit.

Yes, people are incredibly important to any business. But the only difference between the Apple employee group and a mob is: 1) the culture under which people operate; 2) member selection; and 3) incentives.

As a business owner, you are the leader and you're very much in control of the culture, team member selection and incentives. And all of these things are part of your business system. So let's learn how to make your systems better so you can run your business more like Apple and less like a dangerous, unruly mob.

Chapter 2

Systemize

The first step is to systemize your business. The truth is, you're already working some kind of system. You must understand your system as it is now, and then improve it.

First, we're going to create a mindmap of our key business areas: marketing, operations, financial management and customer service.

Second, we're going to make sure we have the right measurement systems in place to keep track of our progress and catch any minor business problems before they become major problems.

Third, we're going to improve our systems by clarifying them into clear, concise, delegable tasks and then find the best person or machine to manage that task.

Systemizing Marketing Processes

Every year millions of businesses fail because of poor marketing. If you're great at marketing, you'll always be able to make money. Without good marketing, you'll always be struggling just to get by. But if you spend 90% of your time marketing just to bring in new and repeat customers, you won't have time left to do other important business tasks. That's why systemizing your marketing is so crucial to your success!

Once you create a marketing system for your business that constantly brings in more profit by attracting new and repeat customers, your job is to let that system continue to work and either improve it or create additional marketing systems. The business with the most effective marketing systems will attract the most customers, all else being equal.

MAPPING YOUR MARKETING SYSTEM

Right now, grab a piece of paper and pen and map your marketing processes. Write down every single component of your marketing and how they all fit together. It doesn't have to be perfect or even beautiful. It just has to have all your different marketing strategies in one place.

You can use traditional mind-mapping with circles and rectangles or just create a list. Whatever works best for you to get all your marketing ideas and processes in one place.

On the next page is an example of my Marketing System Map for my book *Rules of the Rich*.[1]

---

[1] http://amzn.com/B007QMHT5O

The purpose of this mind map is to get all your marketing ideas and strategies in one place so that you can systemize it, improve it and transcend it. It lets you see the forest of your overall marketing power instead getting stuck in the little trees. It's okay to have a lot of little trees if they all add up to a big, powerful forest. But it doesn't matter how big one of your trees is if the forest is disorganized or falling down.

Once you've created your mind map, it's time to start measuring and using analytics.

MEASURING

Want to grow your business? Start being more organized and keep track of the key numbers or Key Performance Indicators (KPIs) of your business. That alone will grow your business significantly. What you measure will improve. What you ignore will get worse. That's just how the human mind works.

The problem is, most entrepreneurs are too "busy" running their business that they fail to accurately and effectively measure what's truly important. That's why little things start falling through the cracks—an employee stealing money that no one notices or a poorly thought out policy that's causing old customers to switch to a competitor. After enough little things fall through the cracks, the big things start to go with it—key customers or members of the team leave, and it's all downhill from there.

What most entrepreneurs need is a little forethought and planning based on sound data. That's why measuring KPIs is so important.

Since most of my business is done online, using analytics like Google Analytics and bit.ly are crucial to measuring my marketing and results. Regardless of what business you're in, make sure you find a way to measure your marketing based on results! How many leads did you get from FaceBook? How many of those leads turned into customers? How much money did those customers spend? Ask these same questions for EVERY marketing strategy on your Marketing System Map.

KEY QUESTIONS TO ASK

- *?* *How many leads did you get from [marketing strategy]?*
- *?* *How many of those leads turned into customers?*
- *?* *How much money did those customers spend?*
- *?* *What is the Life-Time Value (LTV) of your customer?*

Once you have the answers to these questions, you can calculate whether or not a certain marketing strategy is profitable. Sometimes you may want to actually continue unprofitable marketing strategies if you think they will be more profitable long-term. I know it sounds crazy, but here's why:

In some businesses, there are huge benefits to having a certain critical mass of customers. For example, some of the side benefits of having more customers include more referrals, more word-of-mouth marketing, more references, more testimonials, increased credibility, and much more.

So if you have to spend $1.50 to earn $1 in sales, sometimes it's worth it if the net effect is that your business grows. Because if you pay $1,500 in marketing to get a $1,000 sale and then that customer refers one new customer to you at $1,000, you've just made a $500 profit by *overspending* on marketing!

So don't just do a back-of-the-napkin calculation to decide if a certain marketing strategy is truly profitable or not. Think about all the benefits and costs, not just the ones that are easy to measure. Obviously, it doesn't make sense to pay $1.50 to earn $1 in sales for every business. So make sure you understand your business and metrics well enough to make the best marketing decisions for you.

SYSTEMIZING

Now that you've mapped out your marketing strategies and started measuring them, it's time to systemize your marketing even further by breaking down each of your marketing processes into specific tasks. Tasks are the basic units of activity that can be assigned to other people for delegation or a tool for automation.

Here's an example from my *Rules of the Rich* marketing campaign:

Task: Rules of the Rich FaceBook Posting

Post the link to my book on my FaceBook fan page with text that says something similar to:

Learn how to create financial freedom and retire in 3-5 years. My new book Rules of the Rich *is now available on Amazon.com for only $3.97 for a limited time! Grab your copy here:* **http://amzn.to/UFaR1N**

That's a basic task broken down so that anyone can now do that task. Of course, you might need to include more information such as the FaceBook account login information or admin access, the URL of the fan page, what time(s) to post, how often to post, whether or not to promote the post, responding to comments, etc. But this is a simplified version.

You want to simplify ALL of your business tasks so that they can be automated or delegated. Without a system, it's just you clicking buttons and making phone calls. With a system, anyone, anywhere in the world, can operate your business for you—so you can have fun on the beach and still have your business grow every month!

> **ACTION STEPS**
>
> Right now, write out the systems for your major business processes. This includes your marketing strategies from your Marketing System Map as well as any Operations, Financial or Customer Service tasks. It will probably take you several hours to do all of this so start with the MOST IMPORTANT tasks firsts.
>
> *cont/d...*

> Start with the tasks that are so important, you couldn't imagine not doing them every day.
>
> Make sure you do this now so that you can effectively automate and delegate these tasks because that's what we're covering next.
>
> **Note:** People follow what you do, not what you say. Therefore, if you want your employees to help create systems that will help your business grow, you better be setting a good example by creating good systems yourself!

SYSTEMIZING FINANCIAL MANAGEMENT

The financial management of your business can be systemized as well with fantastic results if done properly.

MAPPING YOUR SYSTEM

You should have already mapped out your financial management system, but if you haven't then just do it right now. Get out a piece of paper and map your financial management system. Write down every single task and process of your financial system. It doesn't have to be perfect or even beautiful. It just has to have all your different financial management action steps in one place.

Many common financial management tasks include paying employees, paying contracts, paying the owner, transferring cash into a savings account, transferring cash into a tax account, organizing financial data, bank statements and credit cards, reporting financial data on a monthly, weekly or daily basis, collecting payments due from customers, paying bills, paying suppliers, making investments in new equipment, software or other assets, and other financial transactions.

SYSTEMIZING

Now that you've mapped out your financial tasks, it's time to organize them into clear tasks just as we did with your marketing system.

For example:

- ➢ "Pay American Express credit card every month on the 1st of the month."
- ➢ "Write a check or direct deposit payment to Jean for $1,700 every two weeks on the 1st and 15th of the month."
- ➢ "Transfer $4,000 direct deposit to owner every month on the 1st of the month."

Make sure your tasks are very clear and include financial numbers if at all possible. In the beginning, you'll want to manage every single financial transaction in your business but as you grow you may want to delegate these tasks to others. But even if you never delegate financial management, you ought to at least systemize it so that you never make a mistake. Missing a credit card payment or not paying a vendor can cost you to lose a lot of money simply from being disorganized. Always remember that organized money attracts more money.

FINANCIAL MANAGEMENT TOOLS AND TIPS

I recommend setting your business credit card(s) to automatic payment every month. This will save you a lot of time logging in and paying your bills and will ensure you avoid any late fees or missed payments.

Likewise, I recommend setting up an automatic withdraw every month from your business account to your personal account or savings. This saves time and also helps ensure you're getting paid each month and building wealth. If you don't have personal savings and something happens to your business, you're screwed! If you have personal savings and your business is struggling financially, at least you'll have the ability to fund the business for a while if you want. There's no risk in saving so save as much as you can!

How To Buy Better Services

When it comes to negotiating contracts with employees, contractors, suppliers and others, I highly recommend having some rules to protect you from making a poor decision.

For example, I have a few rules in business:

1) Always get at least 3 quotes for any service or contract that costs more than $500. This ensures you are getting the best deal, or at least a fair deal, instead of getting ripped off by not understanding the market price for the service or product you're purchasing. I see a lot of entrepreneurs hire the first web designer or graphic designer they talk to. That's a huge mistake!

2) Always get at least 3 quotes for any significant expenses.

3) Never pay in full upfront for a service unless it's absolutely necessary. Once you pay in full for something, the other party has lost a huge incentive to deliver high quality work on time. It's a lot harder to get a web designer, for example, to finish your website quickly if you paid them in full than if you still owe them a lot of money. That's just basic human psychology.

4) Ensure all contracts have strict monetary penalties should the other party be late in delivering or keeping to the agreement's time schedule. This ensures you are duly compensated for any delays caused by the other party which could severely damage your business.

RECOMMENDED FINANCIAL MANAGEMENT TOOLS

Here are some great financial management tools that may help as well:

Mint.com[2] is an awesome site that allows you to track all your financial accounts online in a single place. Mint.com will also create charts and diagrams for you as well as budgets, goals and other useful tools to keep track of your finances and plan for the future. I highly recommend it!

CreditKarma.com[3] is an awesome free site that gives you access to your credit score and other personal finance information. This can be important when applying for business loans, a mortgage or a car loan (although I don't recommend taking an auto loan because you're better off paying cash or buying a cheaper car and saving or investing the rest of your cash). Lots of other sites say they provide free credit scores and don't. This one actually does which is why I recommend and use it.

> **ACTION STEPS**
>
> Set up any business credit cards or bills as automatic payments if possible. This will save you a lot of time and hassle and avoid missing any bills.
>
> Create a simple and effective measurement tool or spreadsheet to keep track of the major financial numbers in your company including revenue, Cost of Goods Sold (COGS), overhead, profit and other key financial numbers for your specific business.

---

[2] http://www.mint.com
[3] http://www.creditkarma.com

Systemizing Operations

Mapping Your System

Right now, get out a piece of paper and map your operations system. Write down every single task and process of your business operations. It doesn't have to be perfect or even beautiful. It just has to include all your different operational processes in one place.

Operations vary greatly from one business to another so I hesitate to give examples other than from my own business. Here are some operational processes my publishing company performs: negotiating and signing contracts with clients, editing books, formatting books for Kindle, formatting books for Paperback, publishing books on Kindle and CreateSpace, etc.

Measuring

Operations is often the easiest part of the business to measure, and most business owners do this naturally. This would include counting inventory, measuring how many meals your restaurant served or how many t-shirts your company manufactured.

The key is to measure both your operational inputs and outputs. For a manufacturer, inputs would include raw materials and employee hours and outputs would include the finished products and any waste.

> **ACTION STEPS**
>
> Measure your operational inputs and outputs. Try to maximize your outputs while minimizing your inputs. This means getting rid of excess waste and improving your operational processes to improve productivity and efficiency.

Note: I know all this sounds very basic. It is! These are the fundamentals of running a business. Entrepreneurs who get rich do so by mastering these fundamentals. So get focused on understanding, implementing and improving your operational business tasks. It is the surest, although the least sexy, way to get rich.

Systemizing Customer Service

Systemizing customer service is probably the simplest of all because there's often not very many steps involved. However, being simple doesn't mean it's easy! Often, it's hard to provide excellent customer service because most people are not used to being kind, gracious, compassionate and giving on a regular basis. But these are exactly the qualities that make a customer service worker great at their job! Furthermore, the natural human tendency is to look out for our own best interest and not necessarily the interests of others. A good customer service person must be able to see the world from the customer's point of view.

Remember, your customer service is one of the most important business processes and you should still spend a good deal of time thinking about how to improve your customer service system.

Typical processes include answering customer phone calls and emails, providing an FAQ, providing tutorials or training videos for customers, creating and managing a customer support forum, responding to customer requests on Twitter and FaceBook, etc.

Mapping Your System

How do your customers interact with your company? Every time they do is an opportunity to provide even better customer service. Map out every possible way your customers may interact with your company to build your mind map.

Then, think of how you can improve all these interactions by streamlining them. For example, how can you make it easier, simpler and faster for your customers to get what they want? This could include adding your company contact info to every page of your website or making it easier for customers to call or email your customer service staff to get help with a problem.

Always remember that your customers value time as much, if not more, than they value their money. So anything you can do to save them time will keep them happy, loyal customers and keep their frustration with any problems to a minimum. Real customer service fiascos often occur simply because the customer had to struggle for a long time trying to find a solution, trying to find the company's contact info or waiting on hold on the phone. Don't let that happen to your customers! Good service many times means quick service.

MEASURING

Measuring the effectiveness of your customer service can be difficult to do. But that doesn't mean you shouldn't do it! Everything important should be measured in business, and customer service is certainly no exception.

Here are some good ways of measuring customer service that you may not have thought of or implemented before:

1) Send your customers a survey after they purchase to see how happy they are with your service. Don't make your surveys any longer than 5 questions and make sure you let them know it's a very short survey and provide a bonus or gift for customers who take the time to help you out. You can offer a free downloadable report or a coupon or discount on future purchases, whatever works for your business.

2) Have your team save every positive email or testimonial from your customers, regardless of where they came from (Twitter,

FaceBook, email, survey, etc.). Then, measure every month how many were received. You want a steadily increasing stream of positive reviews and testimonials for your business. If you had 5 such positive testimonials last month and only 1 this month, I would call that a huge warning sign. Look into it and see what could have caused the big drop; was it a drop in customer service quality or did you stop asking for testimonials and sending surveys?

> **ACTION STEPS**
>
> Start improving your customer service pipeline and interactions. Even tiny, miniscule improvements that save your customers just a few seconds can greatly improve customer satisfaction and goodwill–meaning more happy customers and more referrals.

Systemizing R&D

In my publishing company, I'm the chief of Research and Development. That means I'm in charge of coming up with new ideas to grow the business and spotting new opportunities for growth. Of course, I encourage all members of my team to contribute new ideas, spot new opportunities and solve problems. But, at the end of the day, it's my responsibility, and no one cares more about this area of the business than me!

For most lifestyle entrepreneurs, that's just how things are. So what are you doing to improve your R&D? How are you investing in yourself? How are you investing in future ideas and opportunities for your business?

How I Do It

I'm just going to show you how I invest in R&D and maybe you'll find some of these strategies useful for yourself.

Self-Education

I invest a massive amount of time and money in educating myself. I read about 300 books a year, attend several business or industry conferences a year, am a member of several high-level mastermind groups, and I'm constantly watching educational videos online to learn more and grow individually as well as an entrepreneur.

Did you know there are over a BILLION hours of business and educational videos on YouTube available for free 24/7? And yet entrepreneurs don't even watch them? Jim Rohn would say, *"Why do you suppose that is?"*

I think there are a couple of reasons why most entrepreneurs don't watch these free videos. First of all, you're too busy. Instead of organizing and systemizing your business, you spend all your time working in your business, doing the same mundane tasks over and over. So your business never really grows and you never have time to invest in education and R&D. Secondly, you might not know where to look for the right educational material. If you don't have friends like me who spend thousands of hours a year educating themselves about business and separate the great content from the great mass of poor content, you're missing out! I've learned about some of the greatest books, videos and ideas from fellow entrepreneurs who shared them with me in a FaceBook group, phone call, meeting or at a conference. Surround yourself with serious entrepreneurs and they will help point you in the direction of some great resources for education. If you're not hanging around with successful business owners, how do you expect to be successful in business all by yourself?

My Favorite Educational Resources

Here I'm going to share with you some of my absolute favorite educational resources that I believe should be mandatory for every entrepreneur:

TED[4] is an incredible resource of thousands of experts sharing their greatest insights from years of work in 20 minutes or less on video. The business videos are often fantastic but I also find great insights personally from videos that are totally unrelated to business as well.

Jim Rohn[5] was one of the early leaders in the field of personal development. He has passed on, but his legacy is extraordinary. If I were you, I'd start by watching every video of Jim on YouTube.

John DeMartini[6] was featured in *The Secret*. He has been speaking over 300 days a year for many years. He's incredibly wise, and wealthy.

Keith Cunningham[7] once had a net worth of around $100 million in the real estate business, then lost it all when real estate crashed. He's since built it all back and now teaches business skills and tools to entrepreneurs.

Peak Potentials Training[8] was founded by T. Harv Eker. This company has some incredibly powerful business and mental training programs like the Millionaire Mind Intensive, which is a free 3-day course on mastering money by mastering your mind first and foremost.

---

[4] http://www.ted.com
[5] http://www.jimrohn.com
[6] https://drdemartini.com
[7] http://keystothevault.com
[8] http://bit.ly/O3cseo

Landmark Education[9] is a powerful educational curriculum for people who want to create something new in the world, like a business.

CEO Space[10] is one of the world's largest trade show and educational workshop for entrepreneurs. If you want to meet high-level entrepreneurs and investors and learn from the best business advisors, this is the place to go.

MEASURING

Very few entrepreneurs I know actually measure their R&D and investments in self-education, but I do! And I think this one simple strategy has kept me at the top of my game in business. Here's why...

Human beings are programmed to live in a state called homeostasis–a state of balance and familiarity. Our blood and body physiology live in homeostasis and so do our minds and perceptions. That's why you could be earning $100,000 a month right now, and just a few years ago you were earning $100,000 a year. But despite your massive increase in income, you still feel the same financial struggles, worries and anxieties and you still don't *feel* like you're as far ahead as you wanted to be. Why is this? It's because of homeostasis. Your mind adjusts to all new conditions, and it does so very rapidly.

The problem with this constant adjustment to our conditions is that huge improvements in our life don't tend to make huge improvements in our happiness or enjoyment in life. We forget all our past accomplishments and become only interested in our future goals and plans! This can create a cycle of unhappiness and disillusionment. And what's the point of getting rich and being unhappy? That's certainly not what I want for my life!

---

[9] http://www.landmarkeducation.com
[10] http://ceospaceinternational.com

Furthermore, this phenomenon can make us forget what created our success in the first place–which, most of the time, is closely tied to our R&D and investments in our own self-education. This is why many entrepreneurs will study hard for years, create a few million dollars of wealth, and then lose everything a few years later. It's often because the entrepreneur got lazy and forgot what made them successful in the first place.

So how do we avoid this unhappiness trap and the mistake of forgetting the key tasks that make us successful? Here's how I've done it:

Write down a list of every single accomplishment you've ever had in your life that you're proud of. This could be anything from a good grade you got in school to an income or net worth goal you reached to kind words of encouragement from a family member, friend or respected colleague. Don't stop writing until you're so inspired by your list that you can feel the gratitude in every core of your being.

I keep my master list in an Evernote file so I have access to it on every computer, smartphone and tablet I have. That way, I can look at it on a regular basis to remind me of how far I've come and how grateful I am for my life.

Having this list and reading it regularly does several important things:

- ☑ It keeps me grateful
- ☑ It keeps me humble
- ☑ It keeps me inspired
- ☑ It keeps me happily focused on my success instead of worrying about my current problems and challenges
- ☑ It reminds me of what it took to create that success in my life

ACTION STEPS

Start now to develop the habit of learning new ideas every single day. Study videos, books, and educational programs. Don't just study one topic, like marketing. Instead, use a multi-disciplinary approach as Charlie Munger recommends.

Spend at least an hour a day with successful people, preferably people who are far ahead of you in terms of the success you wish to achieve, whether in business or any other area of life.

Write down and create your own accomplishments list. Update it when you achieve new significant goals and read it daily when you're feeling unmotivated or down. It will keep you humble, grateful and focused on what's important.

CHAPTER 3

AUTOMATE

The next step after systemizing your business is automating it. Ideally, you want to automate everything you can while still keeping the same high quality of marketing power, financial management, operational excellent and great customer service.

Some tasks, in my opinion, should never be automated. Things like answering the phone (seriously, no one likes talking to an automated robot on the phone—if a customer has a problem, they want to talk to a person not a machine). Other tasks will actually be much better when automated because automation guarantees it happens whereas humans sometimes make mistakes. A good example of this would include email autoresponders. It would be impossible (and ludicrous) for me to hire an employee or contractor to send out the tens of thousands of emails I send every month through my autoresponder series with Aweber.

So the key here is to figure out which tasks should be automated and which shouldn't be.

> **ACTION STEPS**
>
> Get a piece of paper. Draw a line through the center. Write "Automate" on the left side and "Not" on the right side.
>
> Then, list every task that could potentially be automated without harming your business on the left and write every task that should never be automated on the right.

Here's an example of my automate/not automate tasks for marketing *Rules of the Rich:*

Automate	Not
Tweeting (Tweet Adder)	Facebook Posts
FB Posts Post to Twitter	LinkedIn
Email Autoresponders	Pinterest
FB Posts → LinkedIn	Blogging
	Guest blogging
	Radio
	Finding JV Partners
	Forum Posting
	Podcasts
	StumbleUpon
	Reddit
	Delicious
	Press Releases
	YouTube Videos

The marketing tasks I'll be automating include: Tweeting regularly using TweetAdder[11], having all my posts on FaceBook automatically post to twitter and LinkedIn, and my email autoresponder series promoting the book.

You might think, "Oh, wow, automating 4 marketing tasks. Big deal! That's not going to make much of a difference." Yes it will. Automating those 4 tasks probably saves me over 10 hours a week, if not more. Imagine what you could do with an extra 10 hours a week. And, if you have employees, you will be saving yourself thousands of dollars a month by automating tasks like these. If you can have a machine do something more cheaply and effectively than a human can, you ought to automate it!

OTHER WAYS TO AUTOMATE

There are other ways you can automate your business that you've probably never thought of before. Here are some of my favorite:

CREATE AN FAQ

I get hundreds of emails a month from readers asking the same questions over and over again about self-publishing and marketing books. After typing the same answers over and over again, wasting dozens of hours of valuable time, I finally created a Kindle Publishing and Marketing FAQ on my blog. I wasn't smart enough to figure out how to handle so many emails myself so I asked for advice and my friend and incredible consultant Todd Herman[12] gave me the idea of creating a customer FAQ and having me or my assistant respond to the questions by directing customers to the FAQ (if and only if it helped solve their problem or answer their question).

---

[11] http://bit.ly/NAVZ0s
[12] http://www.thepeakathlete.com/about

Now, whenever someone emails me a question that's answered in the FAQ, I just have my assistant or myself respond with a simple email and link to the FAQ, something like:

> *Hi John,*
>
> *Thanks for your note! I've already answered that question and several others that I think you will really learn a lot from in the Kindle Publishing and Marketing FAQ:* **tckpublishing.com/kindle-publishing-faq**[13]
>
> *If you have any other questions you need help with that haven't been answered there, let me know! I'm happy to help* ☺
>
> *To your success,*
>
> *Tom*

This process does several wonderful things: it saves me a lot of time, saves my readers time, provides a TON of value to my readers, attracts tons of traffic to my blog, gives me insight into what problems my customers are having and how I might improve my service/product for them, and it gives me valuable content that I can use for future videos, books, courses, webinars and other resources.

CREATE TRAINING VIDEOS

Another amazing way to automate parts of your business is by creating training videos. In the emails I was getting from readers, I noticed dozens that requested help in ways which were very difficult to explain in writing—for example, in-depth questions about what buttons to push 8 steps into publishing a book on Kindle. Instead of wracking my brain trying to answer each of these questions clearly in

---

[13] http://www.tckpublishing.com/kindle-publishing-faq

writing, I simply created several free training videos that walk my customer through the entire process from step 1 to the final step.

I then linked to the free video trainings in the FAQ and refer customers to it when they ask a question that's answered in the videos. I'm also using the free video trainings to collect emails to build my Autoresponder database and send even more awesome, valuable content to my customers. It's better for customers and it's better for business.

You can see the video trainings as an example here: eBookpublishingschool.com[14]

> **ACTION STEPS**
>
> Automate anything that a machine can do as well or better than a person.
>
> Don't waste time answering the same questions over and over, especially via email. Instead, every time you get a question, answer it as completely and clearly as possible for the customer. Then, copy and paste that answer into an FAQ on your blog or website and direct future customers who ask the same question to the FAQ.

---

[14] http://www.eBookpublishingschool.com

Chapter 4

Delegate

Now that you've automated as much as you can, it's time to start building your team and delegating the right tasks to the right people at the right time (as soon as possible!).

How To Hire Outsourcers and Contractors

If you've never hired contractors before to do work for you, how do you do it? I get asked this question all the time so I'm going to break down my system for you and hope it will save you the thousands of dollars and hundreds of hours of wasted time and productivity that not knowing this information cost me when I was first building my business team.

Where To Find Contractors

I use Guru.com, Elance.com and Craigslist as I find these are the best places to get many contractor candidates in a few days for free. You can also use vWorker.com. You can use Craigslist US or Craigslist Philippines. Regardless of how you find a contractor, you will need to interview dozens of them to find the right fit for your company and your needs. If you think the first person you talk to will be the perfect fit, whether they were a referral or you found them on a random dating website, you'll probably end up having made a big mistake!

In business, we must make intellectual decisions, not emotional decisions. And you can't make an intelligent decision about a new member of your team without interviewing several people to get an understanding of different personalities, prices, opportunities and challenges. Instead of getting so excited that you hire the first person you talk to, get excited about the opportunity to interview several potential new team members and find the one who will be the best fit for your company. That's using your emotions intelligently.

What To Do

Before you start to choose candidates, you must first plan out your new addition of a team member by asking these questions:

- **?** What key tasks or outcomes will this person or company be responsible for?
- **?** What's my budget?
- **?** What is the price range of this kind of work?
- **?** Do I need a team member who lives in my country, my city or anywhere in the world?
- **?** What special skills or qualities does my team member need to succeed?

Once you figure out what tasks and outcomes are needed, what your budget is, the market price range for that kind of work and the location and skills your ideal team member needs, you're ready to start finding candidates.

Here are some rules I use when hiring contractors:

- ☑ Find as many candidates as possible by posting on multiple sites and accepting multiple applications
- ☑ Always interview in person or via Skype or phone if at all possible. Seeing someone's face and hearing their voice gives you more information than just emailing.
- ☑ If you get a bad feeling about someone, don't hire them. Listen to your intuition.
- ☑ If someone is very slow to respond via email or phone calls, don't hire them. If they're slow to respond now, guess what's going to happen when you're paying them? Yeah, not much.
- ☑ Ask for 3 references and call them if possible. This is especially important the more you're paying. Never pay thousands of dollars for ANYTHING in business without multiple references and doing some serious due diligence. Spending thousands of dollars without doing your research is a good way to go broke faster.
- ☑ Look for reasons to exclude candidates. If you have too many candidates to interview, look for easy reasons to exclude them. This might be a lack of references, poor response time, lack of experience or anything else that might indicate they're not the right candidate for the job.

SELECTING

Once you've interviewed the best candidates, select the one you like best. If it's a very close call between two or more, then test each one out with one task and see who performs it better and responds faster. I'd rather have a good worker with an AMAZING work ethic than an amazingly skilled worker with a good work ethic most of the time.

ALWAYS HAVE BACKUP

Once you've hired a contractor for a particular project or on an ongoing basis, it's absolutely imperative that you have backup! I've seen too many people with an "online business" who have only one website management person. What happens to your business if he gets sick, dies or ignores your emails while he's on vacation? It dies!

Make sure you always have a backup. Don't ever think that with 7 billion people on this planet there's only one web designer or virtual assistant or graphic designer. There are MILLIONS of highly talented people who are happy to work for you for a decent pay. Ideally, you should have someone you've already been in contact with for backup, but if not then just use Guru, Elance or Craigslist to find someone ASAP if your old contractor doesn't deliver.

Never let a contractor hold up your business! This is your business, and you must run it like a serious business. There should be no waiting around for weeks for a contractor. They either get the job done professionally and on time or you find someone else. Period. That's how you run a business. Anything else is charity, which is a wonderful thing, but it's not business.

Another important aspect of this systemization process you're learning is that if and when a contractor backs out on you, you will have the exact directions and instructions to send the new contractor—you can just copy and paste the system for the new person. That makes transitioning jobs or tasks from one person to another as seamless as possible. If you have a great system in place and an employee quits, no big deal. But if you have no system and an employee quits, along with all the knowledge and know-how of their job tasks, you have to hire someone new *and have them start the job from scratch with no clear instructions and crucial knowledge from your company's past experience.*

Delegating Not Abdicating

Before you start delegating tasks, you have to understand how to do it while empowering your team members and yourself. First, let me make a distinction here for you that is VERY important:

> *You want to delegate tasks to your team not abdicate your responsibility to run your business.*

Here's the difference—someone who delegates responsibly will allow members of the team to complete the task and will periodically review the effectiveness of the work. Someone who abdicates responsibility will tell other people to do the work and forget about it, never again checking or ensuring that the work is being done properly. This is how employees embezzle money from their employers, and how companies go bankrupt because no one is ultimately responsible for the business—the owner(s) and/or manager(s) abdicated responsibility and important things fell through the cracks. The key is to delegate wisely so that all of the crucial business processes get done as well as they can or should be done.

In order to delegate effectively you need:

1) Clear Communication

When you delegate a task, you ought to write it as well as speak it, either in person or on the phone. Often, we can communicate by speaking certain details that might be missed in writing. Likewise, we might forget to mention a point or someone might forget a point if we just talk about it without having anything written down.

In nature, there is a universal principle called redundancy. For example, you have two arms, two legs, two eyes and two kidneys. Why? You really don't need two of them—you could survive just fine with only one arm, one leg, one eye or one kidney. But nature has redundancy because it ensures survival. Having two eyes allows you to lose one and still have the other one working just fine. That protects you from being incapacitated by a single injury. Likewise, having redundancies in your business will keep your business from from failing due to a single mistake. This is especially important when it comes to communicating work responsibilities and tasks. Make sure to communicate what needs to be done more than once, without micromanaging and getting in your team's way.

2) CLEAR MEASUREMENT TOOLS AND PROCESSES

After you communicate the task, it's crucial to communicate how you will be measuring the effectiveness of the work. For example, I delegate certain book promotion tasks to my Virtual Assistant. It's basic, routine work that involves posting my books on certain book listing sites and forums. I've communicated ahead of time that I'll be checking to make sure that the correct information is being posted at the correct times.

For other, more complex tasks, you might want to measure things differently. For example, if you have a salesperson on staff, you don't want to measure unimportant things like how far they drive in their car. You want to measure the good stuff—how many sales calls they made, how much they sold and the profit they brought to your company. Let them know ahead of time what you're measuring so that they can succeed according to your goals and expectations. Delegating a task without communicating how you'll be measuring is a good way to set up your team for failure. Don't do that!

3) Clear Feedback Both Ways

Finally, you should ensure clear feedback in both directions. That means, if your team member has a problem, they can email or call you right away and feel free to do so. Or, they can report to someone else in the company. Likewise, you ought to contact them and give them clear feedback on how they're doing, any changes that need to be made and any other important information they might need from you to do the job.

The Best Use Rule

The Best Use Rule is a very simple one—you should always be spending your time in the most productive, efficient and effective manner. One of the biggest areas where people fail to apply this rule is in simple, mundane or routine tasks.

For example, let's say your business earns you a profit of $10,000 a month and you work 100 hours a month. That means you earn $100 an hour. Therefore, any tasks which could be delegated, outsourced or automated for less than $100 an hour should be taken off your plate so you can focus on high-value activities.

If you want to grow your business, you absolutely must focus only on the highest value activities you perform. Everything else must be automated, delegated, systemized or, in the worst case scenario, ignored. Therefore, if you can get someone to do laundry for you for $10 an hour, you should. If you can get someone to cook meals for you for $20 an hour, you should. If you can get someone to do mundane marketing tasks for you for $5 an hour, you should.

And, in many cases, you ought to be delegating tasks that cost up to $100 an hour or even more. This is because of what economists call comparative advantage. Comparative advantage is when two people or entities can gain advantage through trading, even though one party may be more efficient in each area. For example, you may be a better social media marketer and a better business manager than your employee. However, since managing your business is a more valuable activity financially, it makes sense to pay your employee to manage social media, even though they will do a worse job than you. This is because you gain a huge comparative advantage by focusing more of your time and resources on managing the business, and can therefore profit more from this arrangement. Not taking into account comparative advantage is a huge mistake many business owners make, and it will keep you from seizing huge opportunities for profit.

The problem for most new entrepreneurs is that they're not earning enough money to feel like they can afford to outsource such tasks. So what happens? They stay stuck and their business doesn't grow. Trust me, that's what I did for two years!

Then, one month I decided I would hire a full-time Virtual Assistant from the Philippines for $350 a month, even though I wasn't sure how I was going to pay for it and still have enough money to pay my bills. Five months later, I had increased my income by five times! As soon as I outsourced all the mundane, routine tasks, I finally had enough time to focus on the most important parts of my business—creating great products for my customers and marketing.

Then, I was finally earning enough money to feel like I could pay for someone to clean my house, do my laundry, make meals, and I became an outsourcing fanatic. Once you see the results from delegating and systemizing your business, you will NEVER go back! If you think you are the one who should be doing mundane business tasks all day then your business will never grow. Once you learn to delegate, your business will grow by leaps and bounds. Well, that's what happened for me at least.

Systemization Phase 1

Research

Most people want to skip research and go straight to action. *"Okay Tom, I'm leaving my business for a year. Let's systemize it!"* you might think. Hold that thought!

Before we systemize anything, it's important to do your homework upfront. Contrary to popular opinion, great businesses and great successes in life don't happen because of luck or chance. Most of the time, they happen because of world-class preparation, research and planning backed up by a whole lot of implementation. But the preparation, research and planning must come first. Now it's time to start researching your business.

Customer Research

What's the greatest asset of your business?

Some people would say Intellectual Property—maybe your books or systems or processes or copyrights or patents.

Others might say the entrepreneur and CEO—you can't have a business without an entrepreneur creating and a business manager driving it.

Others have told me that employees are the most important asset. At the end of the day, your business goes home with your employees, and if they don't show up to work tomorrow, you've got some problems.

While each of these areas are important and crucial to any successful business, in my humble opinion they are not the most important part of the business. Your customers are. Because, trust me, if you've built your business in a certain way, you could fire your employees, take a year off work, fail to protect your intellectual property and still make one hell of a profit if you have happy customers. You couldn't do that forever, but you could do it for at least a year.

On the other hand, you could have everything else in place, but without your customers, you wouldn't earn a dime of profit.

But your customers aren't just the wonderful people who pay your bills and create a profit for your business. They're also the greatest source of information you could ever ask for. All you have to do is ask your customers and they will tell you what they want!

It's not always what they say that counts, it might be how they say it. But, if you're smart about it, you'll find out from your customers how to grow your business 10 times or more by giving them more of what they want.

Here's how to find out what your customers want.

Getting The Goods From Your Customers

It's time to get the goods from your customers. The goods, in this case, are the information that you need to keep your customers happy for life and attract new customers. And all you have to do to get that information is ask!

Survey Your Customers

The first thing you can do is survey your customers. You can create a fast, free and simple survey with SurveyMonkey.[15]

Ask your customers questions like these:

- **?** *What do you love most about (your company, product or service)?*
- **?** *What do you dislike most about (your company, product or service)?*
- **?** *Why did you buy from us?*
- **?** *How could we improve our product or service to make you happier?*
- **?** *What is your biggest problem in life right now that you think we might be able to help you with in some way?*

Listen To Your Customers

Besides surveying your customers, you can start *listening* to your customers. Here's what I mean. You want to look for the *exact language* your customers are using when they talk about your company, your products and the customer's problems.

---

[15] http://www.surveymonkey.com

Realize that your business only exists because it helps customers solve their problems. But they won't buy from you unless they understand *ahead of time* how you will help them solve their problem. If you use the exact language your customers use when they talk about their problems in your marketing materials, they will think, "Wow! This company gets me. That's the exact problem I'm having. They must be able to help!"

Consider these two marketing headlines:

How To Systemize, Automate and Delegate Your Business So You Can Spend More Time on Vacation

How To Grow Your Business By Working Less and Traveling More

On the surface, both of these headlines might sound just fine to you. You might think they're both good and would probably be just as effective. But that's not true!

The first headline is the words I personally use and thought of. The second headline includes the words my customers use. Big difference!

My ideal customer for this book is always talking about how they want to "work less and travel more." They don't say "I would like to spend more time on vacation" in emails, conversations and FaceBook posts nearly as often as they say "work less and travel more." That's an example of using your customer's words.

And I can guarantee that 90% of the time or more, when you use your customer's words in your headlines and marketing materials, your sales will go up. Why? Because your customers KNOW those words—those are their words. Those are the words floating around in your customer's mind. And when you use their words, they like you more! And when they like you more, they're more likely to buy from you.

What You Can't Mess Up

Let me share with you some of the results from my research about what you MUST include in your business processes before taking a business vacation.

Customer Service

Customer service is the most important part of ANY business. I don't care what business you're in! Taking care of your customers and turning one-time orders into life-long customer relationships will do more for your business than a million brand new customers who never order again.

My mentor Keith Cunningham drilled this question into my head and it stuck. Stick it in your head, too:

> *"How much money would your business be making if you kept all the customers you've ever had?"*

When I did the math, I realized I had lost MILLIONS of dollars worth of life-long customers because of poor customer service and just not caring enough! And I didn't even notice. I was so busy chasing new customers that I lost millions of dollars in lifetime sales by not taking care of the customers I already had.

Do everything you can to keep your customers. If you're going to be gone from your business, make sure you have someone with a GREAT attitude who's very kind and well-trained to deliver EXCELLENT customer service while you're gone.

If you could only make one investment to improve your business for life, 90% of the time. it should be an investment in improving customer service.

Systemization Phase 2

Plan

Now that you've done your research, it's time to plan your strategy. It might be tempting to just go ahead and start implementing new processes in your business right away, and I commend you on your enthusiasm to do so. Just realize that a few minutes of planning will save you hours of time when it comes to implementation.

Furthermore, the planning could save you from numerous problems down the road which come about as a result of taking action before thinking things through.

The best way I've found to plan is through a process of asking and answering key questions. Below are some of the most powerful questions I've found and used to grow my businesses.

Questions To Ask For Planning

What Kinds of Massive Value Am I Going to Create for My Customers?

At the end of the day, your business revenue will be based on the value you provide for your customers. The more value you provide, the more money you make. If you want to increase your sales, the surest way is to either help your current customers even more by providing more value or to take your value and provide it to more new customers.

Just one small idea on raising the value of your product or service could take your business to a whole new level of growth and profitability. Constantly ask yourself, "how can I add more value to my customers?"

What Systems and Resources Do I Need To Grow?

This is one of the crucial questions that many entrepreneurs and freelancers fail to ask and understand. In order to grow from, say $5,000 a month in sales to $50,000 a month in sales, you have to have an entirely *different* system in place (for most businesses). This is often the stage where a solo-entrepreneur must now bring on new team members, either employees or contractors, to grow the business. And the skills it takes to build and manage a team are entirely different from the skills it takes to work as a solo-entrepreneur or freelancer. Systems are what make the difference, and the systems only come about as a result of the entrepreneur carefully planning and designing them.

Whose Help Do I Need To Achieve My Plan?

This is another crucial question to ask. I guarantee you one thing—if you knew how to grow your business from where you are to where you want to go, you would have done it already. The problem is, most often, a lack of skills or knowledge. But I can also guarantee you that there's someone out there right now who has the skills and knowledge you need to grow your business to that next level. Finding those people and getting them to become an advisor, mentor or consultant is the fastest way to grow your business—assuming you actually take that knowledge and skills and do what it takes to grow to the next level.

Adding More Value

Here are some of the strategies I used to add a lot more value to my customers.

Create A Free Video Training Course

I've created free training courses for customers in my target market. eBookPublishingSchool.com[16] for example, targets the ideal market for readers of my Kindle Publishing Bible book series. On that site, I give out 4 free training videos that teach authors and publishers how to create and publish bestselling books on Kindle.

Create A Free eBook

Creating a free eBook is a fantastic way to add more value to your target market, and it works for almost any business. The idea is that you create a free eBook educating your target customers about *how to solve an important problem.* For example, if you sell jewelry, I would

---

[16] http://www.eBookpublishingschool.com

highly recommend giving away an eBook that teaches your target customers how to care for the kind of jewelry you sell. It would teach all the basics of cleaning and polishing silver, caring for gold jewelry, how to store jewelry, how to keep jewelry safe while traveling, and anything else that would be helpful to your customers.

This strategy is incredibly effective for a number of reasons. First of all, reciprocity is a major psychological trigger for buying. Giving away a free gift triggers reciprocity from your customers. Second, adding massive value to your customers for free makes them value your paid products or services even more. They think, "Wow! If this is what I get for free from this company, imagine what I'll get when I actually buy something." And that's how you grow a business very quickly—by providing massive value.

CREATE A LIST OF RESOURCES FOR FREE

Resources that solve your customers' problems are also fantastic for attracting new customers and keeping your old customers happy and satisfied. You could create a list of contacts for your jewelry customers—for everything from jewelry cleaning to safety deposit boxes to insurance agents that specialize in insuring luxury jewelry. This simple list would only take a day, at most, to create—yet the benefits it would yield in terms of customer loyalty would be astounding. Imagine if you are a wealthy woman who has been buying jewelry for 50 years. You've probably spent a few million dollars on jewelry in your life. Then, one day you buy a gold bracelet from a small jewelry shop. No big deal, just a few thousand dollars. But with your new bracelet, you get a sheet of paper giving you names, phone numbers, emails, and websites of trusted people you can go to for help with all your other needs that relate to jewelry—storage, insurance, cleaning, etc. What kind of impression would that make on you? Chances are, you'd tell all your friends not about that little bracelet you bought, but about the incredible service you got from that little jewelry store that went the extra mile and did something different.

This kind of strategy is helpful to your success in any business. But it's CRUCIAL to your success in a commodity business. For example, if you sell life insurance or a similar commoditized product or service, this kind of extra offering is the only way you can truly differentiate yourself from the competition. And if you do it right, they won't be talking about your product—they'll be telling their friends about your incredible service and how you go the extra mile for your customers. That's how you grow a business rapidly from referrals.

CREATE A VALUABLE AUTORESPONDER SERIES

Autoresponders are such a powerful way to connect with your customers. Autoresponders are email management systems that allow you to send out emails on a regular basis based on when someone signs up for your email list to get your free eBook or other offer.

Despite its incredible effectiveness, few small businesses use email marketing. And even fewer use email marketing in a way that produces enough sales to justify the cost of implementing email marketing (both in terms of time and money). Here's how to create a killer autoresponder series that will help your customers and help you by attracting more sales:

1) Offer something that helps your target customer solve a problem in exchange for the customer opting in to your email marketing list.

2) Create a series of at least 5 to 10 followup emails that create a closer relationship with the customer. These emails *must* be either helpful, informative, interesting, funny, or noteworthy in some way. If your emails are boring or look like spammy corporate newsletters, your customers won't read them.

3) Offer to provide an even better, different or more comprehensive solution to your customer's problems by selling them one of your products or services. This should *not* be done in a "salesy" way. Instead, you should frame it so that the customer sees buying your product as a very helpful, simple and worthwhile solution to their problem.

If you've never used an Autoresponder before, I recommend Aweber[17] because they have great 24-hour customer service and are very reliable.

---

[17] http://aweber.com/?375818

Systemization Phase 3

Implement

Now it's time to implement your plan. By now, you're probably so excited about all the changes and potential for growth that you're ready to go. If that's how you feel then great! You can put the book down right now and start implementing.

If, however, you're feeling nervous, stuck, anxious or fearful about making these changes, it's time to take another look at why that might be. What's holding you back from making changes? What changes seem fun and easy to make and which ones seem difficult or impossible?

Sometimes we feel overwhelmed because *it seems like there's so much to do and not enough time to do it all.* This is a skewed perspective of reality and it leads to procrastination, frustration, and failure.

Instead, *focus on what you can do right now!* Just take *one step forward at a time.* That's all that is required for success. Just take that next step. Just implement that one thing that you can do right now to improve your business. Once you're done with implementing step 1, you can choose to move on to step 2 whenever you want—or not—it's up to you. Just make sure you take that first step!

Systemization Phase 4

Review

Okay, you've done your research, created your plan, implemented your plan and now you've got an entirely new or expanded product, value funnel and promotion and added TONS of value to your customers. You're done, right?

No way!

What separates great entrepreneurs from good ones is the simple habit of going the extra mile. What you've done so far is only just round one! You might make two, three, four or five hundred rounds of doing this same process over and over again, improving it every time as you learn more and more what your customers want and how to add even more value to their lives.

I can guarantee that if you've followed this process thoroughly and done Phases 1 through 3, you've now learned A TON of information that you didn't know before. Go sit down right now and use that information to do an EVEN better job of helping your customers.

Massive Value Bonuses For Your Customers

Now it's time to come up with even more massive value bonuses for your customers. *"Even more?"* you ask. Yes! Even more.

You want to add so much value to your customer's lives that they would have to be INSANE, CRAZY or JUST PLAIN STUPID to do business with anyone else.

Testing and Preparing

One key point here is that you ought to be testing and preparing your business BEFORE you leave! It's important to let your contractors, employees and systems run without you before you leave so that you can test and tweak them before you go on vacation. This way, you'll be able to test for any initial problems and either train your people to overcome those problems or tweak your system to solve the problems.

This is the opposite of what most business owners do. Most business owners will give full responsibility to their employees or contractors when they're gone, and then when they return home they're upset because mistakes were made and not corrected. How foolish! Why not just give your people and systems more responsibility to run the business without you BEFORE you leave? That way, you'll be around to help fix the problems and correct any mistakes. Then, when you do leave for real, your systems and people will be able to manage it without major problems.

Systemization Phase 5

Repeat

Feel free to repeat Phases 1-4 as needed. This should be a never-ending process for your business of constantly finding new ways to automate and delegate tasks to even higher levels of efficiency and quality.

Your goal should be to improve efficiency and quality every single year in your business. If you don't, your competitors will and they will crush you. If you do, you'll be one of the few, the proud and the courageous entrepreneurs who succeed long-term.

Chapter 5

Solving The Big Problems After Systemization

A lot of business books I've read give great advice and tools on how to solve a particular problem, but then fail to show you how to solve the problems that happen AFTER you solve the problem.

The truth is, you will always have problems. Once you solve the major problems plaguing most entrepreneurs and freelancers of not having enough money and not having enough time to grow the business, will your life really get any easier? Yes and no.

Yes, your life will get easier because you'll finally have enough money to pay all your bills, make some upgrades in your lifestyle and save and invest money for the future. You might use that extra money to buy a new car, a new house or take a vacation all around the world like I'm doing as I write these words overlooking a gorgeous pool and courtyard in the Philippine islands. It's great to have money to buy nice things and not have to worry about paying the bills. But it's even better to have the time to enjoy it as well!

I'm sorry to disappoint you, but I must say that overall your life won't get much easier once you systemize and grow your business. Instead, your life will get *different.* You'll have different problems once you solve the problems you now have. Instead of worrying about how to pay your bills, you'll be worrying about how to grow your company to the next level or how to safely and profitably invest all that extra cash. Yes, once you solve the problems you now have, you'll simply be graduating to a new school of life with new and hopefully more challenging problems. That's how you grow, and the more you grow, the better life gets. But I can't say it really gets "easier."

Part of this phenomenon I'm describing here is called the Hedonic Treadmill. It's the basic human cycle of striving to achieve a goal or objective, getting it, and then setting a new, higher goal or objective. The problem with this cycle is that it can be extremely frustrating when we get what we want and find out we're still not happy.

This happens to people every single day. The Hedonic Treadmill isn't just some fancy word for an academic theory—it's human design. We're programmed biologically to constantly strive for more, better and different. Hence the old saying, "The grass is always greener on the other side." We always want that next big thing. But then when we get it, we're not nearly as happy, fulfilled or excited as we though we would be.

Should you be lucky, intelligent and diligent enough to systemize, automate and delegate your business well, you will finally achieve your goal of having a certain amount of money or traveling the world or retiring early, whatever your goal is. I just thought I would warn you that having the business and lifestyle you've always dreamed about isn't necessarily as good as you've always dreamed it to be.

Now that's not to say that achieving your dreams isn't worth it. On the contrary, I believe achieving your dreams is the one of the *only things* in life that's truly worth the effort.

I just hope that these words of warning will keep you from a mid-life crisis or depression when you find out that getting what you've always wanted just leads to you wanting more. It's a wonderful thing to achieve success—but if you're not happy, fulfilled and grateful for your life right now, I'm not at all sure that getting what you want will solve those particular problems.

Okay, enough with philosophy. Let's learn about some of the most powerful tools any entrepreneur can use to systemize, automate and delegate.

Chapter 6

Ninja Business Tools and Tricks

Here you'll find my ultimate toolkit of productivity and business tools that allow me to systemize, automate and delegate tasks, saving hundreds of hours a month. Use these tools wisely!

Scheduling

Google Calendar[18] is my favorite calendar and scheduler. You can keep track of all your appointments and meetings with it, and it will even send reminders to others if you want. Google Calendar will also sync with any smartphone to send you reminders about your appointments. You can also set it up to get email notification reminders about appointments. You'll never forget an appointment again—even when traveling internationally!

You might also want to use a physical calendar or scheduler as a backup just in case.

---

[18] https://www.google.com/calendar

Project Management Tools

Basecamp[19] is a powerful project management tool that is simple, easy to use and works very well. Highly recommended for medium to large organizations with numerous team projects.

Surveys

SurveyMonkey[20] is a great way to create quick and easy surveys for your customers.

Scheduling Apps

One of the best ways to save time is by not scheduling unnecessary appointments or meetings. But we all have to schedule things, so why not use a scheduling app that helps save you time when making appointments?

Doodle[21] and **ScheduleOnce**[22] are both great free scheduling applications.

Email Autoresponders

Aweber[23] is the service I use and I like it the best in terms of their customer service, deliverability and quality.

---

[19] http://basecamp.com
[20] http://www.surveymonkey.com
[21] http://www.doodle.com
[22] http://www.scheduleonce.com
[23] http://aweber.com/?375818

MailChimp[24] has a free offering but I never recommend it because it's got serious limitations for serious marketers and is not nearly as scalable as other autoresponders.

ConstantContact[25] works well and is a close 2nd to Aweber in my opinion.

Mad Mimi[26] is a new kid on the block and has a free program which I haven't used but I hear is better than MailChimp according to some internet marketing colleagues.

GOOGLE PLUS+ VIDEO HANGOUTS

A **Google Plus+ Video Hangout** is an awesome way to create a free "webinar" or class online. It's absolutely free to use and you can record it and upload it to YouTube with the push of a button. It's an awesome way to record online classes, web TV interviews and 1-1 coaching sessions with clients.

EMAIL AUTO-RESPONSE

With Gmail or other webmail program. Create a FUN, ENTERTAINING, INTERESTING and VALUABLE auto-response. You WANT people to read it and like it.

---

[24] http://mailchimp.com/
[25] http://www.constantcontact.com/
[26] https://madmimi.com/

For example, I wrote:

> "Hey,
>
> You're not going to believe this, but right now I'm sipping Mai Thais on the beautiful beaches of Thailand. Or maybe I'm swimming with penguins in South Africa. Well, either way, I'm doing this crazy 90-day trip around the world with my fiancé and it's pretty awesome. Heck, who am I kidding, IT ROCKS! I'm having the best time of my life!
>
> And want to know the cool part? My business is growing even faster now that I'm gone than it was when I was working very day at home.
>
> Want to know how I'm earning more money by NOT working than I was when I was working every day? I'm going to share all these lifestyle and business secrets with you in my new book Systemize, Automate, Delegate.
>
> You can get on the special waiting list here to get a sneak peek of what it's all about: LINK
>
> Make today the best day ever!
>
> To your success,
>
> Tom Corson-Knowles
>
> Wow, you read this whole email? Good for you! You deserve a 3-month vacation too! Get yours here: [LINK]"

Email Management

Boomerang[27] is a very helpful app for Gmail users. You can use it to keep track of email conversations and remind yourself to follow up with people if you don't hear from them after a certain period of time. You'll never lose track of a new prospect or important conversation again if you use Boomerang.

Streak[28] is an awesome Customer Relationship Manager (CRM) software that will plugin with your email system and allow you to keep track of customers as well as send emails in the future which can be handy.

Unroll.me[29] is an awesome service that will help you reduce email overload. I use Unroll which will sort all your newsletters, let you unsubscribe from them and then combine all unnecessary emails from senders you choose to be sent only one time per day in one large email compiled with each individual email inside it. So instead of getting 15 unimportant emails all day long, you get the one "Rollup" from Unroll and you can keep your inbox cleaner while still having access to those emails that *might* be important at some point.

USE GMAIL FOR FILTERS

I use Gmail for email because it's just awesome. It will store an almost unlimited number of emails (I've never had a problem storing my hundreds of thousands of emails over the last 5 years).

Another awesome thing with Gmail is that it will let you filter emails before they ever reach your inbox. Here's how you can use this filtering tool:

---

[27] http://www.boomeranggmail.com
[28] http://www.streak.com
[29] http://unroll.me

AUTOMATICALLY DELETE ANY EMAILS FROM CERTAIN SENDERS OR THAT CONTAIN CERTAIN WORDS OR SUBJECT LINES.

I use this function to delete any spam messages I get from people who have newsletters without an unsubscribe button and people who send out chain letters, political emails or other time-wasters.

AUTOMATICALLY ADD CERTAIN TYPES OF EMAILS TO FOLDERS FOR LATER USE

I often get updates about my business or other issues through email, and many of these messages just aren't important when they're sent. Examples include training video courses or newsletters from internet marketing experts or competitors. I can store all these in a separate folder using Gmail filters and then they never reach my inbox—they go straight to a folder that I can view later when I need them.

STAY AWAY FROM UNNECESSARY NEWSLETTERS

Unsubscribe from any email lists that are not absolutely necessary. Or create a filter and send them to a folder that you can check whenever you want. That way your inbox won't be cluttered with marketing from other businesses.

CLEAR IT TO ZERO

If you've never cleared your inbox down to zero emails, now's the time to do it! Use the tools I've mentioned before like Unroll.me and Gmail filters to make it easier. And then clean out the clutter! With Gmail, you can just archive old messages and find them later so you don't have to delete everything to clean out your inbox. But at least clean out your inbox! Trust me, if you haven't done anything important with those emails in the last month or the last year, it's time to get it out of your inbox.

You'll feel a lot better when your email is finally manageable instead of feeling overwhelmed every time you check it.

OTHER WAYS TO SAVE TIME ON EMAIL

Have your team members only email you about important problems and opportunities. Team members should never be emailing you about simple things that they could easily Google or figure out on their own. I once had a team member email me to ask the definition of a word he didn't understand. It would have saved us both time if he had just Googled it. Train your team to treat your time and their time as precious, and to be proactive about solving problems. Otherwise, you'll be the only person in your business solving problems, creating a decision-making bottleneck. That's no way to run a business.

Don't check your email first thing in the morning. Instead, write down your work priorities for the day and do your most important tasks in the morning. Then check email later in the day or at night when it's less likely people will respond to you immediately, allowing you to clear your inbox much faster.

Another awesome tip I learned from Tim Ferriss is to empower your employees to make customer service decisions below a certain cost threshold. For example, if a customer wants a refund or has a problem, your team should be able to handle it without asking you for permission as long as it doesn't cost over a certain amount of money, maybe $50, $100 or $500 depending on the size and scale of your business. This saves you a lot of time having to confirm refunds on a small $22 order when you could be spending that time bringing in big new clients or relaxing on the beach. It will also provide your customers with better service because your team will be able to respond and help them faster without waiting for your decision.

Voicemail Management

Google Voice[30] is an amazing tool that makes voicemail so much easier to manage, especially when you're traveling. With Google Voice, you can listen to voicemail messages in any order instead of clicking through like a normal voicemail box which is a waste of time. It will also automatically transcribe voicemails to text so you can save a lot of time reading them. It can also send you an email notification of new voicemails and you can listen to them on your computer or any tablet as well as your phone. If you're in another country with no cell service, Google Voice is invaluable!

Skype

Skype[31] is mandatory. If you don't have it, get it now. It's free and you can communicate with people all over the world via Skype. When you're traveling internationally, you can call back those people who left a voicemail in your Google Voice inbox too! The vast majority of my meetings and phone calls are now done through Skype and it allows me to work with an international group of people just about as easily as working with someone in my home town. The only thing you have to manage is time zone differences!

Outsourcing / Team Building

Guru.com[32] is a my favorite site for finding contractors on a budget. You'll have to go through a lot of applicants to find a good fit, but that's the case any time you add a new member to your team. I love Guru because you can simply use Guru to find and recruit a team member and then communicate with them outside of the site. With many other

---

[30] https://www.google.com/voice#inbox
[31] http://www.skype.com
[32] http://www.guru.com

similar sites, you are forced to communicate and pay only through that site which does not lend itself to building a sustainable, long-term business team because there's a third-party in the way.

Elance.com[33] is a good site to find contractors for small jobs, but you're forced to communicate and pay through Elance, making it more work to manage and not my first choice.

vWorker.com[34] is another site similar to Elance.

Craigslist[35] is a good site to find contractors and new team members. The downside is all the spam that comes with posting on Craigslist.

PASSWORD MANAGEMENT

1Password[36] is a great password management tool that syncs across all computers and mobile devices. It will save you time trying to remember all your passwords.

Roboform Password[37] management is another great tool for storing all your passwords automatically for you.

FILE STORING, SHARING AND BACKUP

Dropbox[38] is an awesome free service for storing files in a cloud server. It will sync across all devices and computers and makes it very easy to share files with friends and team members. You might want to pay to upgrade for more space if you need a lot of storage. You can also use it to back up important business files and documents.

---

[33] https://www.elance.com
[34] http://www.vworker.com/
[35] https://www.craigslist.org/about/sites
[36] https://agilebits.com/onepassword
[37] http://www.roboform.com
[38] http://db.tt/5UMxnvsE

Evernote[39] is an amazing piece of free software that you can use on any computer, tablet or smartphone. You can use it for keeping track of notes, documents and all kinds of important business information. It syncs across all devices and is incredibly easy to use with some amazing advanced features that will save you a lot of time and money.

Document Scanning Apps

There are dozens of free and paid apps for any Android or iPhone that you can use to scan, store and send documents such as contracts. All you do is snap a picture of each page and the app will save it, turn it into a PDF and email it anywhere you want as well as store a copy on your phone just in case. Right now, I use **GeniusScan**[40] for my iPhone (it's free).

Voice Recording / Notes

I use voice recording frequently to capture ideas, thoughts, and information much faster than I could type or write it. It's especially great when you wake up in the middle of the night with an idea and want to record it fast.

QuickVoice[41] is a free iPhone app that allows you to take voice notes.

Time Zones

If you're on the computer, worldtimezone.com[42] is a great fast, easy way to find out what time zones people are in and set appointments.

---

[39] http://evernote.com
[40] http://thegrizzlylabs.com/
[41] https://itunes.apple.com/en/app/quickvoice-recorder/id284675296?mt=8
[42] http://www.worldtimezone.com/

World Clock-Time Zones[43] is a great iPhone app for this when you're on the go

For Android users, just search in the app store for a World Clock or Time Zone Converter.

TEXT AUTOMATORS

Auto Hotkey[44] is totally free for PC. Instead of retyping large strings of text you frequently use for emails or other computer work, you can use a text automator to sore these words and then copy/paste them quickly and easily.

BUILDING WEBSITES

I've created a free video training series that will teach you how to build your own professional Wordpress website in about 30 minutes for less than $75. Check it out at BlogBusinessSchool.com[45]

RESOURCES:

Wordpress is the [free] system I use to build my websites.

GoDaddy[46] is what I use for buying domain names. I love their 24-hour customer service.

BlueHost[47] is what I use for website hosting. I also love their 24-hour customer service.

---

[43] https://itunes.apple.com/us/app/world-clock-time-zones/id403693694?mt=8
[44] http://www.autohotkey.com
[45] http://www.blogbusinessschool.com/
[46] http://www.tkqlhce.com/click-5271137-10378406
[47] http://www.bluehost.com/track/tcorsonk

Optimize Press[48] is an amazing Theme for Wordpress that allows you to create amazing Squeeze pages, sales pages, and membership sites very quickly and easily. There's a little bit of a learning curve, but if you're familiar with Wordpress, you'll find it pretty easy to create awesome marketing tools and marketing funnels for your business.

Chris Farrell Membership Site[49] is the best community I've ever seen for asking questions and getting advice on how to build websites and grow an online business.

Creating Valuable Content For Customers

YouTube[50] is awesome for uploading videos and embedding them on your website.

Vimeo[51] is another good option for uploading and embedding videos on your site.

Easy Webinar Plugin[52] is a plugin for WordPress that allows you to create a beautiful evergreen webinar to sell products or services or just to educate your audience. You can get a free trial which allows you to create one custom webinar with custom landing pages and the webinar will run every day if you want it to. It's great for anyone who's selling products online!

Camtasia[53] (for Mac or PC) is an amazing piece of screen recording software and video editing software all in one. With it, you can create amazing sales videos, educational videos, and give easy, clear, fast

---

[48] http://nanacast.com/vp/97647/39530/
[49] http://juicetom.farrell10.hop.clickbank.net/
[50] http://www.youtube.com
[51] http://vimeo.com
[52] http://a5969g13i6yfrvb31ql9ku5r45.hop.clickbank.net/?tid=BOOK
[53] http://www.techsmith.com/camtasia.html

instructions to your team members by recording videos of your computer screen while you work or teach.

Screenflow[54] is another great screen recording software and is cheaper than Camtasia but only works for Macs right now.

SOCIAL MEDIA

TweetAdder[55] is an awesome tool for automating a lot of Tweeting as well as getting a ton of new targeted Twitter followers.

HootSuite[56] is a great tool for scheduling Tweets and managing multiple Twitter accounts at once.

Buffer[57] is a great tool for auto-scheduling Tweets with 1-click. You'll also find some great suggested Tweets that work nicely as well.

IFTTT[58] (IF This Then That) is a great tool for automating social media posting and book marketing across various platforms. I highly recommend testing it out to see how it can help you save time on manually posting social media updates.

> *Here's one of my favorite IFTTT "recipes"—it automatically sends every email I star * in Gmail to Evernote, thereby storing it. This helps clear my inbox*

---

[54] http://www.telestream.net/screenflow/overview.htm
[55] http://www.tweetadder.com/idevaffiliate/idevaffiliate.php?id=15532_0_1_6
[56] http://hootsuite.com/
[57] https://bufferapp.com/app
[58] https://ifttt.com/

Mechanical Turk

MTurk[59] is an incredibly powerful service that can be used in some really creative ways. Basically, with MTurk you can hire thousands of people to do short tasks that may last a few seconds or minutes for pennies.

Miscellaneous

CallControl[60] for Android. This app blocks all calls to your cell phone from callers that have been marked as spammers.

AirBNB App[61]. Helps when traveling to find a place to stay quickly and easily if you'd prefer to stay in a home rather than a hotel.

Photoshop[62] is an amazing tool for creating graphics quickly and easily for those of you who have any interest or skill at design. Even if you don't, it's a good skill to learn. If you never create a design in your life, at least knowing how to will give you a better eye for what good design looks like and how to hire the right designers.

Microsoft Excel is a great tool for organizing data or running any major calculations or analytics for your business. Learning how to use Excel was probably the most important thing I learned in business school other than accounting.

Dragon Naturally Speaking[63] is a great tool for dictating. For slow typists, this one program could dramatically improve your typing speed and output.

FreeMind[64] is a great free tool for mind mapping.

---

[59] https://www.mturk.com/mturk/welcome
[60] https://play.google.com/store/apps/details?id=com.flexaspect.android.everycallcontrol&hl=en
[61] https://www.airbnb.co.uk/mobile
[62] http://www.photoshop.com
[63] http://amzn.com/B008MR36FE

Computer Organization

When you look at someone's desktop, you can immediately tell whether or not they're an organized person.

Here's a good example of a horribly organized computer desktop:

Your desktop doesn't have to be perfectly immaculate but it should be clearly and neatly organized and you should be able to easily and quickly find anything you need for your business or personal life as soon as you look at your desktop. Here are some tips for organizing it:

Create a folder for every major business project. If you have several projects such as managing a website or writing a book, create a folder for each of those projects. Then, every picture, file or document that's a part of that project goes in the file, neatly organized.

Next, create a folder for every type of reoccurring file or document. For example, I have a file for publishing contracts. All the contracts go in that file to keep them organized. If I ever need to refer back to one, it takes 10 seconds to find it.

---

[64] http://freemind.sourceforge.net

Next, delete any outdated or unnecessary files. If you have multiple versions of a book, for example, delete all the old, outdated versions to save space and keep things organized. This will also save you a lot of time instead of accidentally writing new information in an outdated file and then having to fix everything afterwards. Organization saves a lot of time if you do it right.

Bonuses!

Free Video Course for Growing Your Business

As a special "thank you" for buying this book, I want give you free access to my entire *Systemize, Automate, Delegate* video training course where we cover the lessons in this book in even more detail.

You can get free access to the course here (The regular price is $297, and this course is only free for readers!):

https://www.udemy.com/systemize-automate-delegate/?couponCode=SystemizeAutomateDelegate

Special FaceBook Group

Come join our FaceBook group just for readers like you who want to take their marketing to the next level. In this group we'll be sharing our successes, marketing tips and strategies with each other so that we can all continue to grow our businesses together.

This is also a fantastic group for finding joint venture partners and cross-promotion opportunities! Imagine if you had hundreds of other entrepreneurs from all over the world collaborating with you—imagine how big of an impact you could have.

It's also a great place to get any marketing questions you have answered as well.

Come join us here on FaceBook:

http://on.fb.me/Tsk8ss

Free Blogging for Business Training

If you're a business owner and want to learn how to start a blog for your business that makes a profit, I've developed a free online training program to teach you everything from how to build your blog to getting traffic to monetizing it.

You can get the free training at:

www.BlogBusinessSchool.com

Connect With The Author

Thank you so much for taking the time to read this book. I'm excited for you to start your path to creating the lifestyle of your dreams through growing your business.

If you have any questions of any kind, feel free to contact me directly at: **www.TCKPublishing.com/contact**

If you'd like more free training and info on how to build a profitable online business, visit: **www.BlogBusinessSchool.com**

You can follow me on Twitter: **@JuiceTom**

And connect with me on FaceBook:

http://www.facebook.com/onlineinternetmarketinghelp

You can check out my internet marketing blog for the latest updates here: **http://www.onlineinternetmarketinghelp.com**

I'm wishing you the best of health, happiness, and success!

Here's to you!

Tom Corson-Knowles

About The Author

TOM CORSON-KNOWLES is the #1 Amazon best-selling author of *The Kindle Publishing Bible* and *How To Make Money With Twitter*, among others. He lives in Kapaa, Hawaii. Tom loves educating and inspiring other entrepreneurs to succeed and live their dreams.

Learn more at Amazon.com[65].

---

[65] http://amazon.com/author/business

Other Books By Tom Corson-Knowles

The Book Marketing Bible: 39 Proven Ways to Build Your Author Platform and Promote Your Books on a Budget

Schedule Your Success: How to Master the One Key Habit That Will Transform Every Area of Your Life

You Can't Cheat Success!: How The Little Things You Think Aren't Important Are The Most Important of All

Guest Blogging Goldmine

Rules of the Rich: 28 Proven Strategies for Creating a Healthy, Wealthy and Happy Life and Escaping the Rat Race Once and for AllSystemize, Automate, Delegate: How to Grow a Business While Traveling, on Vacation and Taking Time Off

The Kindle Publishing Bible: How To Sell More Kindle eBooks On Amazon

The Kindle Writing Bible: How To Write a Bestselling Nonfiction Book From Start To Finish

The Kindle Formatting Bible: How To Format Your eBook For Kindle Using Microsoft Word

The Amazon Analytics Bible: How To Use Analytics To Sell More Books

How To Make Money With Twitter

101 Ways To Start A Business For Less Than $1,000

FaceBook For Business Owners: FaceBook Marketing For Fan Page Owners and Small Businesses

INDEX

1

1Password 75

A

Action Steps 14, 18, 19, 22, 27, 30, 33
AirBNB App 80
analytics 11, 12, 80
Android 76, 77, 80
Auto Hotkey 77
autoresponder 29, 31, 55
Aweber 29, 56, 68, 69

B

Basecamp 68
Best Use Rule 41
BlueHost 77
Boomerang 71
budget 36, 37, 74
Buffer 79

C

CallControl 80
Camtasia 78, 79
cash flow 2
CEO Space 25
checklist 5
communicate 40, 74, 75
complacency x
ConstantContact 69
contractors .. 6, 17, 35, 37, 52, 60, 74, 75
Craigslist 36, 38, 75
CreateSpace 19
CreditKarma 18
CRM 71
Cunningham, Keith 24, 49
customer service .. 2, 6, 9, 20, 21, 22, 29, 49, 56, 68, 73, 77

D

decisions 13, 36, 73
delegating 3, 35, 39, 42
DeMartini, John 24
Doodle 68
Dropbox 75

E

Easy Webinar Plugin 78
eBookpublishingschool 33, 53
eBookPublishingSchool 53
effectiveness 21, 39, 40, 55
efficiency 19, 61
Eker, T. Harv 24
Elance 36, 38, 75
employees 4, 5, 6, 15, 17, 31, 39, 46, 52, 60, 73
Entrepreneurs 20
Evernote 26, 76, 79
Excel 80
extra mile 55, 59

F

FaceBook.. 12, 14, 20, 22, 23, 31, 48, 83, 84, 85, 90
FAQ 20, 31, 32, 33
feedback 41
Ferriss, Tim 73
filters 71, 72
Financial management 2
followup emails 55
free eBook 53, 55

G

GeniusScan 76
Gmail 69, 71, 72, 79
GoDaddy 77
Google Calendar 67
Google Plus 69
Google Voice 74
Guru 36, 38, 74

H

Hangout 69
happiness 25, 85
Hedonic Treadmill 64
homeostasis 25
HootSuite 79

I

IFTTT 79
incentives 7
inputs 19

K

Kindle 19, 31, 32, 53, 87, 89

L

landing pages 78
Landmark Education 25
lifestyle .... ix, xi, 22, 63, 64, 70, 85

M

Mad Mimi 69
MailChimp 69

marketing 4, 1, 4, 5, 9, 10, 11, 12, 13, 14, 16, 27, 29, 30, 31, 41, 42, 48, 55, 69, 72, 78, 79, 83, 84, 85
Marketing System Map 10, 12, 14
marketing tools 78
master list 26
membership sites 78
Millionaire Mind Intensive 24
mindmap 9
Mint.com 18
monetizing 84
MTurk 80
Munger, Charlie 27

O

operations 2, 14, 19
Optimize Press 78
organization 4, 5, 6
outcomes 36, 37
outputs 19

P

passwords 75
Peak Potentials Training 24
Photoshop 80
plan 4, 18, 36, 51, 57, 59
priorities 73
problem xi, 12, 21, 25, 29, 31, 41, 42, 47, 48, 53, 55, 56, 63, 64, 71, 73
processes 1, 3, 4, 6, 10, 13, 14, 19, 20, 39, 45, 49, 51
procrastination 57
productivity 19, 35, 67

Q

QuickVoice 76

R

R&D 3, 22, 23, 25, 26
research 37, 45, 49, 51, 59
risk management 6
Roboform 75
Rohn, Jim 23, 24
Rules of the Rich 10, 14, 30, 89

S

sales 3, 4, 13, 40, 48, 49, 52, 55, 78
ScheduleOnce 68
Screenflow 79
Skype 37, 74
social media 1, 42, 79
streak 71
successful people 27
survey 21, 22, 47
SurveyMonkey 47, 68

T

team members 36, 39, 52, 73, 75, 79
TED 24
text automator 77
time zone 74
transcribe 74
TweetAdder 31, 79
Twitter 20, 21, 79, 85, 87, 90

U

Unroll.me 71, 72

V

video training 77, 83
Vimeo 78
Virtual Assistant 40, 42
voice recording 76

W

voicemails 74
vWorker 36, 75

webinar 69, 78
WordPress 78

Y

YouTube 23, 24, 69, 78

www.ingramcontent.com/pod-product-compliance
Lightning Source LLC
Chambersburg PA
CBHW052104070526
44584CB00017B/2334